COMETS
AND
METEORS

COMETS AND METEORS

GEORGE S. FICHTER

A GROLIER COMPANY

FRANKLIN WATTS
NEW YORK/LONDON/TORONTO/SYDNEY/1982
A FIRST BOOK

FRONTIS: COMET IKEYA-SEKI,
NOVEMBER 2, 1965

Cover photograph of Comet Ikeya-Seki
courtesy of Holiday Film Corporation
Interior photographs courtesy of Hansen
Planetarium: pp. ii, 37, 63; n.c.: p. 10; NASA:
pp. 15 and 20; the American Museum of
Natural History: pp. 17, 24, 27, 29, 39,
43, 46, 48 (top and bottom), 51 (photo by
Jean Bratman), 52 (photo by Jean Bratman),
54 (photo by Jean Bratman).

Library of Congress Cataloging in Publication Data

Fichter, George S.
Comets and meteors.

(A First book)
Bibliography: p.
Includes index.
Summary: Defines and describes comets and
meteors, including such famous comets as the
recurring Halley's Comet, and tells how to look
for them.
1. Comets—Juvenile literature.   2. Meteors—
Juvenile literature.   [1. Comets.   2. Meteors.
3. Astronomy]   I. Title.
QB721.5.F5   523.6   81-21887
ISBN 0-531-04382-7   AACR2

CONTENTS

CHAPTER ONE

VISITORS FROM OUTER SPACE

On the night Mark Twain was born in 1835, Halley's Comet rode brightly and majestically across the heavens. Soon afterward the big comet disappeared and was not seen again for seventy-five years. But on the night Mark Twain died in 1910, it coursed the sky again.

Coincidence? Undoubtedly. But some people ascribe special significance to these occurrences.

Mark Twain did not see the comet on either of its visits, but throughout his life he did have a strong interest in comets. Comets were more plentiful in the 1800s than they have been in this century. Once Mark Twain sent an "advertisement" to a New York newspaper proposing a tour of space on Coggia's Comet, which was big and especially spectacular at that time. He priced the seats on his pleasure excursion at two dollars per 50 million miles (80 million km) and guaranteed deluxe accommodations for every passenger. He also offered substantial rate reductions for organized groups that signed up in advance.

According to Mark Twain, the tail of the giant comet could carry as many as a million passengers. Travel aboard the comet would take place along some 100,000 miles (160,000 km) of road, and communication between different parts of the comet would be by telegraph.

Scientists had no way of predicting Mark Twain's time of birth or death, but they did know with reasonable certainty that Halley's Comet would be seen in 1835 and again in 1910. By all calculations, it should come into view again late in 1985 and be at its closest point to the sun in February 1986.

One of the biggest and most beautiful of all comets, Halley's is also one of the most predictable. Records of its appearances date back to 240 B.C.

Like other comets, this monstrous luminous body in the sky has been viewed in the past with awe, fear, and suspicion. Any important events occurring during the year a comet appears are usually attributed to the comet. But every year has its highlights, both good and bad.

William the Conqueror, for example, successfully invaded England in 1066, the year of a visit from Halley's Comet. It was during this same year that England's King Harold was killed in the Battle of Hastings. And when Halley's Comet appeared on schedule in 1456, it is said that the Pope excommunicated it, declaring it to be an agent of the Devil. No other comet has ever attained such prominence.

The Great Comet of 1811 was the largest comet in recorded history. The diameter of its head was estimated to be greater than the sun's diameter. The comet was in view for more than a year and a half, which is an exceptionally long time for a comet to be visible. People in Portugal were certain that the comet was responsible for that year's extraordinarily bountiful crop of good grapes. The Comet Wine made from the 1811 crop was very popular and brought a premium price. The year 1811 also happened to be the year of the worst earthquake ever recorded on the North American continent. Furthermore, the earthquake was centered in Missouri—a most unexpected place for an earthquake to occur.

But were either of these events due to the comet? There is no reason to believe so.

Many people fear comets even today. They are sure that

comets signal disaster. Some even think that comets are a sign that the world is coming to an end. Yet as far as anyone knows, except for one that may have hit Siberia in 1908, no comet has ever struck the earth. A direct hit would unquestionably cause far greater damage than any explosion produced by humans. The chances of such a collision, however, are extremely small.

Despite the immensity of comets, they have surprisingly little substance or mass. They never disturb the orbits of any of the planets past which they travel. To the contrary, the course of a comet may be greatly altered by the gravitational force of the bodies it orbits. Some of the very large comets consist of about the same mass as the smaller ones. The larger ones are simply more spread out. Comets glow due to reflection of light from the sun and a process called *fluorescence.* In fluorescence, ultraviolet rays from the sun are absorbed and then re-emitted as visible light.

Meteors, or more precisely *meteoroids*, are different from comets. They are solid objects traveling through space at great speeds. A bright streak across the sky marks the path of a meteoroid that has encountered the earth's atmosphere. The bright streak itself is called a *meteor.* Meteors glow because they are heated to incandescence by friction.

Most meteoroids are very small. They burn up, or vaporize, while still many miles above the earth. A few of the larger ones do reach the ground. These are called *meteorites.* More than 2,000 meteorites have been found so far. Yet there is only one verified record of a meteorite hitting a person.

It happened on November 30, 1954. Mrs. Ann Hodges was resting on a couch in her living room in Sylacauga, Alabama. Suddenly, she was awakened by a tremendously loud noise that sounded like the explosion of a stick of dynamite. Shocked, Mrs. Hodges jumped to her feet and then noticed a pain in her left hand and hip. On the floor at her feet was a softball-sized rock. She bent down to pick it up, but it was too heavy for her to lift, and it was strangely warm.

Later it was determined that the hit was actually a glancing blow. The meteorite had ripped a hole in the roof and ceiling of the house. It smashed a radio sitting on the table and bounced from there to the couch where Mrs. Hodges was lying. The weight of the meteorite, incidentally, was only 9 pounds (4.05 kg).

Meteors are by far our most frequent visitors from space. If you watch the sky closely at night, away from streetlights, you will see at least one "shooting star" every fifteen minutes. At some times of the year, meteors literally shower from the heavens.

One of the most spectacular meteor showers in recorded history took place on November 12, 1833. All through the night the meteors fell in awesome numbers. They sped across the sky by the countless thousands, like a veritable blizzard. People were absolutely certain—and understandably so—that the sky was falling.

"North America bore the brunt of the display," Agnes Clarke related in her *History of Astronomy in the Nineteenth Century.* "From the Gulf of Mexico to Halifax, until daylight put an end to the display, the sky was scored in every direction with shining tracks and illuminated with majestic fireballs. At Boston the frequency of meteors was estimated to be about half that of flakes of snow in an average snowstorm. Their numbers, while the first fury of their coming lasted, were quite beyond counting; but as it waned, a reckoning was attempted, from which it was computed, on the basis of that much diminished rate, that 240,000 must have been visible during the nine hours they continued to fall." Most meteor showers are less of a show.

A meteor trail

Scientists tell us that some meteoroids are related to comets. These are the ones formed from the solid debris left over when a comet vaporizes in space. Each time a comet passes near the sun, some of its lighter, more gaseous elements evaporate.

The rain of debris onto the earth is constant. Fortunately, most meteorites are dustlike in size. But it is estimated that as much as a hundred tons of this so-called *cosmic dust* falls onto the earth or into the oceans every day! This amounts to about 3 pounds (1.35 kg) per square mile annually. Once it was thought that much of the thick "ooze" covering the floor of the oceans consisted of cosmic dust. Now it is recognized that this material has many sources. Cosmic dust contributes its share, though. We know this because large amounts of nickel—an element especially abundant in cosmic dust—are typically found on the ocean floor.

Much has been learned about comets and meteors in recent years. Some things, however, remain a mystery.

CHAPTER TWO

WHAT ARE COMETS?

Countless billions of comets are believed to travel on aimless and endless journeys through space. In comparison to the vastness of the universe, comets are extremely small chunks of frozen gases. One leading scientist described them as "dirty snowballs." Most have a core, or *nucleus*, made of rocky or metallic substances, but all are very loosely structured.

Aristotle thought that comets were patches of air that caught fire and burned. Of course, this is not true. Most astronomers today believe that they are the bits and pieces left over from the formation of the solar system billions of years ago. The scientist Jon Oort has proposed that the solar system is surrounded by a giant sphere of cometary material (called the *Oort Sphere*), and that every now and then a fragment of this matter leaves its orbit and begins to fall toward the sun. It is this fragment that we see as a comet.

ORBITS OF COMETS

Comets change in character when they enter the solar system and come under the direct and powerful influence of the sun and planets. Some travel in well-defined orbits. Scientists can calculate their paths with accuracy and can tell almost to the day when they will come within viewing distance of the earth. These comets are called *periodic comets*, and their orbits are elliptical, or egg-shaped.

—*13*

Most comets, however, have such eccentric or large orbits that their paths cannot be calculated, or the comet will not return for hundreds or even thousands of years. These are among the many comets that may be seen only once and never again. The time it took for one comet to complete its orbit, for example, was calculated at 24 million years!

Most comets can only be seen during a portion of their orbits, but Schwassmann-Wachmann 1 is always visible from somewhere on earth. It travels between Jupiter and Saturn, and although it is usually faint, it occasionally flares to a surprising brightness. At these times, it can be seen even with a small telescope. Its nearly circular orbit is completed every fifteen years.

Why does the comet sometimes become brighter? Scientists are not sure, but there is some evidence that the flares are brighter whenever there are sunspots.

PARTS OF A COMET

A comet has a head and, usually, a tail. Within the head is a nucleus—small particles of rock, dust, or metals coated with frozen methane, ammonia, carbon dioxide, and other gases. These particles are widely separated. The distance between each is believed to be much greater than the size of the particles themselves. The nucleus of most comets measures no more than several miles (3.2 km) across, although it becomes much larger as the comet gets closer to the sun.

The Comet Kohoutek, photographed by Skylab 4 *on December 25, 1973, using a special ultraviolet (UV) light camera. Note the head and coma of the comet and its tail, which is directed away from the sun.*

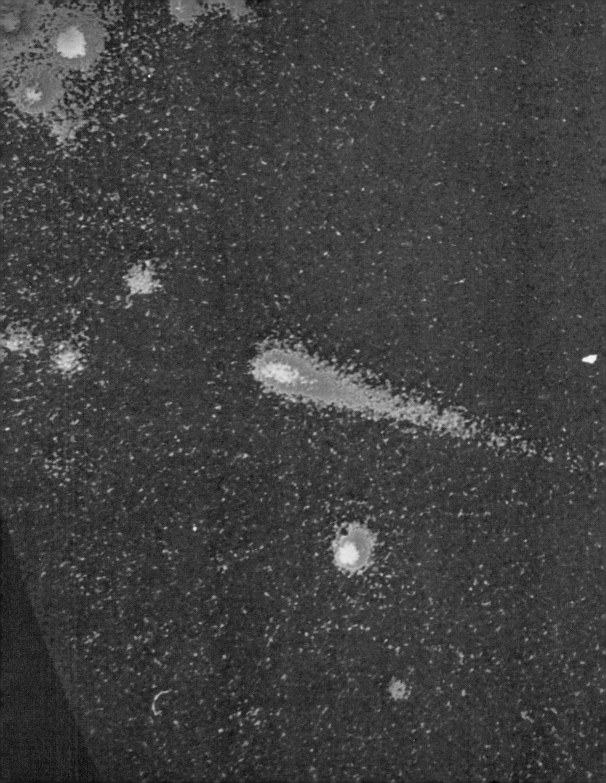

Surrounding the nucleus is the *coma,* a fuzzy cloudlike envelope of gases. The nucleus plus the coma form the head of the comet.

The mass of the comet's nucleus is generally estimated to be less than a millionth of the earth's mass. The coma and tail are even thinner, thinner, in fact, than the best vacuum we can create in our laboratories. An astronomer once described comets as "bags full of nothing."

Because of the many particles it contains, the head of the comet is its brightest part, but the long tail may be more pronounced. At one time, comets were called "hairy stars." The word *comet* refers, in fact, to their long-haired appearance, which presumably resembles a woman's long hair blowing in the wind. Early Chinese astronomers called comets "broom stars."

Some comets become incredibly large. With their tails stretched for hundreds of millions of miles, they can cover half or more of the visible sky. Comets that are still far from the sun generally do not have tails. Fully expanded in orbit closer to the sun, however, a comet's tail is a ghostlike trail. One astronomer said he thought that a million miles of the vaporous material in a comet's tail could easily be fit into an average-sized suitcase.

In 1910, people were filled with fear when astronomers reported that the earth would pass directly through the tail of Halley's Comet. They were especially anxious because the comet's tail was said to contain the deadly gas cyanogen.

The scientists were correct. The earth did indeed pass through the tail of the great comet. However, the air was so misty and the moon so bright on that April 19 night that no one knew precisely when it happened. The gas was there, too. But the earth's atmosphere served as an effective shield against the few widely separated particles. The only harm that came to people that evening was from the stress they brought on themselves in their near panic.

An 1857 drawing showing what some people feared might happen if a comet struck the earth.

Throughout the 4.6 billion years of its existence, the earth may have traveled through the tails of many comets. The only other time on record, though, was in June, 1861, when the earth passed through Tebbutt's Comet. Again, there were no apparent effects.

The gases that form the comet's tail are pushed out from the head and stream behind it, always away from the sun. Typically, the tail is narrowest near the head and fans out broadly to the rear. Because they absorb some of the sun's radiation, the particles of gas in the comet's tail are excited to luminescence. This gives the tail an almost eerie glow.

BRIGHT COMETS

The brightest comets are those that travel close enough to the sun to pick up much of its radiation and reflect its light, but which are far enough away from the sun to avoid being destroyed, or vaporized, by it.

A comet that appeared in 1843 is generally ranked as the brightest comet in historic times. It could be seen clearly during the day, and its tail was estimated to be 300 miles (480 km) long. Another onetime visitor seen over Africa in 1910 was named the Daylight Comet because of its uncommon brightness.

COMET COLORS

Most comets are yellowish or bluish, due to reflection of the sun's light and to the process of fluorescence. A variety of colors have been reported, however. The color seen often depends on the light present, the atmosphere, and the position of the observer. Orange is common and is apparently related to sodium emissions from the head of the comet. One of the most unusual comets ever viewed was the Jarlove-Achmaroc-Hassell Comet of 1939. It was described as a definite green by all who saw it.

HOW COMETS ARE NAMED

Comets are usually named for their discoverers, many of whom are amateur sky observers. One amateur astronomer in Ohio has discovered more than a dozen new comets. If the comet is first seen by two or more observers, all of the names are used in the name of the comet. They are separated by hyphens, as in the Honda-Mrkos-Pajdusakova Comet.

There are some notable exceptions. Halley, for example, did not discover the comet that bears his name. It had been observed many times over the years, but it was Edmund Halley, in 1705, who established the fact that some comets travel on regular orbits in the solar system. The bright periodic comet on which he based his calculations was named in his honor.

Halley predicted that the comet he observed in 1682 would return in 1758. Until then comets had not been considered true members of the solar system. His prediction received little support from other scientists, however. Halley died in 1742, so he did not see the comet's return on Christmas night in 1758. It moved across the sky on the precise path he said it would follow. This was the first time that the orbit and return of a comet had been calculated.

Names for comets can become cumbersome, even difficult. Thus, comets are also cataloged by the year of their appearance and by the order in which they appear during the year. For example, a comet listed as 1983d would be the fourth comet seen during the year 1983.

The elliptical, or oval-shaped, orbits that comets have mean that at one point in its journey a comet is closest to the sun (called *perihelion*) and at another point it is farthest from the sun (called *aphelion*). The first comet each year to have reached "perihelion passage" is named I, the second II, and so on. These Roman numerals are added to the year of its appearance—for example, 1983II. When enough information about a comet's orbit is known—for instance, when that comet's peri-

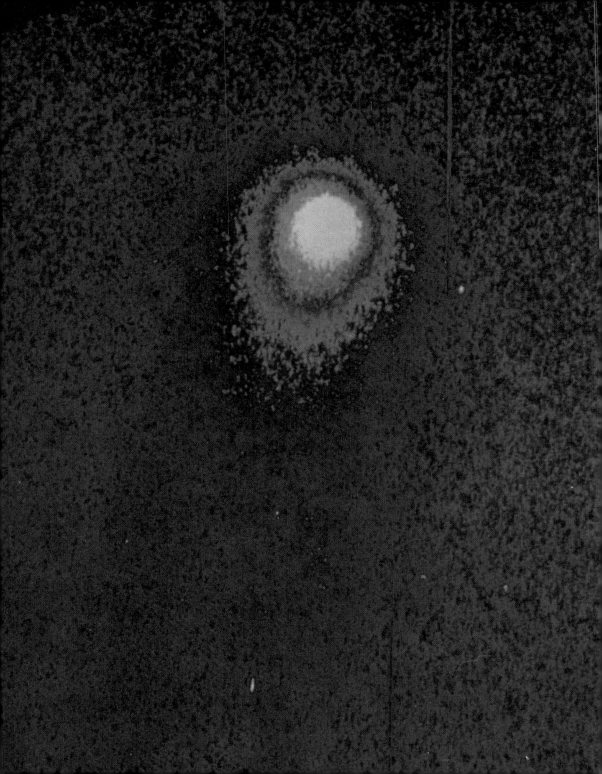

helion passage takes place—the listing for that comet is changed from its order of appearance to its order of perihelion passage. Thus, the fourth comet to appear in 1983, at first named 1983d, could be changed to 1983V if that comet was the fifth in 1983 to pass through its perihelion point.

HYDROGEN CLOUDS
SURROUNDING COMETS

The Tago-Sato-Kosaka Comet of 1969 was the first comet to be observed beyond the earth's atmosphere. With special equipment aboard an orbiting astronomical observatory, it was discovered that the comet was surrounded by a huge hydrogen cloud. This was the first time that free hydrogen had been detected in a comet.

In Bennett's Comet of 1970, it was discovered that this comet was surrounded by a cloud of hydrogen about fifty times larger than the sun. However, the comet itself was only medium-sized. The ejection of the hydrogen was in direct proportion to the speed of the comet in its path around the sun and sometimes caused the comet to go into eccentric motions in its orbit. In addition, hydrogen halos were found around Kohoutek's Comet in 1973–74, and it was noted that the amount of hydrogen increased as the comet came closer to the sun.

COMET DUST

Comet dust has been examined by many scientists. They think that the dust may provide important clues to the formation of

A photograph of Kohoutek taken by Skylab 4, *using a special UV camera and showing the halo of hydrogen surrounding the head of the comet.*

the solar system some 4.6 billion years ago. Great amounts of comet dust fall onto the earth every day, but all of the particles are contaminated, in various ways, as they pass through the earth's atmosphere. To obtain pure dust, *U-2* aircraft were flown at altitudes of 65,000 feet (19,500 m)—above the level of terrestrial pollution. Then dust particles were collected on sticky plates exposed from the aircraft. The plates were sealed immediately and treated with the same care as were the rock samples that were brought back from the moon.

Scientists at the University of Washington and the California Institute of Technology were able to analyze bits of dust that were as small as 1/2,500 of an inch across and that weighed as little as 30 billionths of an ounce. Three kinds of particles were found in the dust. Two were fluffy, indicating that they had never been part of a dense meteoroid. One of these consisted of as many as a million different kinds of minerals. The other was made up of tiny crystals of a single kind of mineral. The third and rarest group of particles consisted of small hard spheres, indicating that they had been formed during a melting process.

The calcium and magnesium in these samples were significantly different from the same elements found in the earth's rocks and minerals. The differences suggest that the dust may have been formed at the time of the solar system's beginning. Scientists want to collect more samples to verify these initial findings.

CHAPTER THREE

SOME FAMOUS COMETS

Many of the numerous comets seen during the 1800s will not return for hundreds of years. Some may never return. These are comets that have large or eccentric orbits. Of the more than six hundred comets that have come within view during historic times, more than seventy have been seen at least twice. More than half a dozen of these have appeared at least a dozen times. From approximately six to a dozen comets—almost half of them new discoveries—are seen every year.

ENCKE'S COMET

Encke's Comet is one of the most notable of the periodic comets. It has made more than fifty observed returns since it was first reported in 1786. Its *period,* or orbiting time around the sun, is only 3.3 years, and this time decreases every century. Apparently it moves closer and closer to the sun on each orbit. Encke's Comet is therefore becoming very dim, and it no longer has enough substance to form a tail. The Wilson-Harrington Comet, first seen in 1949, had an even shorter period—only 2.3 years. But it was seen just once and never again.

When Encke's Comet first came into the solar system—and no one really knows how many years ago this was—it was probably much larger than it is today. Now, you can see Encke's Comet only with a telescope. Each time it comes into

*Encke's Comet, photographed
on October 29, 1914*

view it is dimmer than before. Part of its "fuzz," the coma surrounding the nucleus, has been blown away by the solar wind. Its years are numbered, so to speak.

BIELA'S COMET

Some comets have disappeared after being on a regular orbit for many years. One of the most famous of these is Biela's Comet. Its short orbit of 6.8 years was determined by calculations that were made when the comet was sighted in 1826. The comet did indeed return on schedule in 1832. But in 1839, it could not be seen because it was directly in line with the sun and seemed extraordinarily close.

On its next observable visit, in 1846, Biela's Comet had changed greatly and was surprisingly different in character. Now it had two heads. They were joined in the center by a "bar." This made the comet look very much like a weightlifter's dumbbell. Apparently, the comet had been pulled apart as it neared the sun on its last visit.

Scientists waited anxiously for Biela's Comet to appear in 1852. Would it still have two heads, or would they be joined again as one? Or, on this visit, would the two parts of the comet have separated completely?

Biela's Comet was now two distinct comets traveling side by side—at an estimated 1 million miles (1.6 million km) apart! In 1859, sky conditions were similar to those in 1839, so the comet could not be seen clearly. But in 1866, when viewing conditions were again excellent, Biela's Comet did not appear at all.

Where did it go? The Adromedid meteor showers seen from mid-November through early December of that year are believed to have come from the remnants of Biela's Comet.

DONATI'S COMET

Donati's Comet of 1858 ranks as one of the most beautiful comets of all time. It had three tails—a long, curved main tail and two shorter ones. But three tails? Unusual, yes, but Comet De Chéseaux, observed in late 1743 and early 1744, had six tails! Rough calculations indicate that Donati's Comet will be back again around the year 4000.

Some comets have tail-like "spikes" at the front of their head. These spikes are directed toward rather than away from the sun. The first spiked comet observed was the Arend-Roland Comet of 1957. Another was reported in 1973 when the astronauts aboard the U.S. space station *Skylab 3* got a close look at Kohoutek's Comet from space.

KOHOUTEK'S COMET

Kohoutek's Comet was discovered in 1973 by a Czechoslovakian astronomer. When he detected the comet, it was 600 times fainter than the faintest star visible without a telescope. But it was expected to become a spectacular show for the naked eye and perhaps the most dramatic spectacle of this sort in this century.

Although Kohoutek's Comet did appear on schedule, it did not perform as had been anticipated. It was never bright enough to become a spectacle, like Halley's. Nevertheless, it was probably the best-observed of all comets thus far. Astronomers, both amateur and professional, were alerted and ready for the comet both in space and on the ground. The astronauts on *Skylab 4* drew sketches as they observed the comet through binoculars. When it was seen in its closest position to the sun, the head of the comet was a bright yellow, and its sunward spike was a pale yellow. As the comet moved farther from the sun during the following week, the sunward spike disappeared from view, and the comet's color changed to white tinged with

Donati's Comet,
as pictured in 1858

—26

violet. Scientists detected significant amounts of water vapor plus carbon dioxide and carbon monoxide in its makeup.

Though Kohoutek's Comet did not live up to its advanced billing, it still ranks as the top comet of this century to date. The thrust given to Kohoutek's Comet by Jupiter's gravitational pull, put it into an orbit that will not bring it back for about 75,000 years.

LEXELL'S COMET

Except for the possible hit in Siberia in 1908, the closest any comet has ever come to the earth in recorded history was in 1770. The comet was Lexell's, and its orbit has since been so disturbed by Jupiter's pull that a return is unlikely. But in July 1770, Lexell's Comet came within 1.5 million miles (2.4 million km) of the earth. It appeared to be larger than the moon and was a more awesome sight than any comet before or since. Astronomers note that the comet really had an extremely small mass. Had it been more massive, it would have pulled the earth into a larger orbit and thus changed the length of our year.

HALLEY'S COMET

Halley's Comet is unquestionably the most famous of all the comets. Some historians believe that Halley's Comet is the Christmas star, or star of Bethlehem, depicted in nativity scenes. Almost everyone recognizes the comet's name, and many people are truly surprised to learn that Halley's Comet is just one of many comets that ride through the sky. Half a dozen or more are seen every year. Two or three of these are on well-predicted return visits. But Halley's is well known because it is one of the few that is bright enough to be seen easily with the naked eye. Also, some people have the opportunity to see the comet twice in their lifetime.

European space scientists plan to meet Halley's Comet on its next visit. Using solar-powered engines on an unmanned spacecraft, the emissary launched by the European Space

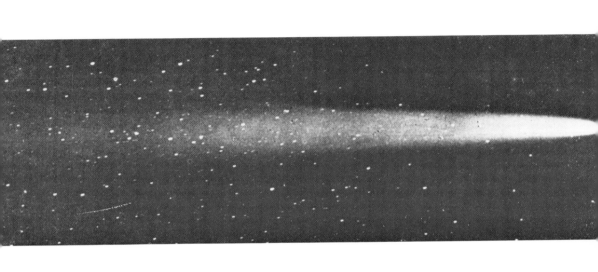

Halley's Comet,
May 15, 1910

Agency is expected to fly alongside the comet as it travels some 75 million miles (120 million km) from the earth. A probe will be dispatched from the spacecraft and will go to within 600 miles (960 km) of the comet's nucleus to take pictures and to record data that will be sent back to earth for analysis. Scientists agree that the spacecraft could be damaged or even destroyed by the debris hurtling around the comet, but the opportunity to come this close to the comet is unparalleled. And Halley's will not return again until 2062!

U.S. scientists hope they might be granted funds for a similar project, for this is a chance for comet research that cannot be duplicated for many years. Some American scientists propose sending their spacecraft from Halley's Comet to a rendezvous with the much smaller Temple 2 Comet in 1988. The spacecraft would fly alongside the comet for at least a year, and if conditions proved favorable, it would be moved to within 60 miles (96 km) of the nucleus and then closer still—to a distance of only 30 miles (48 km). At these locations, it would take aboard gases and dust for analysis and would photograph the comet in detail.

CHAPTER FOUR

LOOKING FOR COMETS

A comet's speed depends on how close it is to the sun. It travels fastest when it is nearest to the sun—its perihelion. It goes slowest at its greatest distance from the sun—its aphelion. Top speeds for comets are somewhere around 300 miles (480 km) per second. Most travel much more slowly, though, at around 20 miles (32 km) per second or less.

However, when you view a comet with your naked eye, or even through a telescope, the comet appears to be almost motionless. Even though its actual speed is as great or even several times greater than the speed of a "shooting star," or meteor, the comet is so far from the earth that its movement is hard to detect unless you watch it for at least several hours. This is partly what makes comet watching so interesting and, in a subtle way, more dramatic than viewing the momentary flash of a meteor. A big, bright comet rides slowly, surely, and majestically across the heavens.

Some professional astronomers make the study of comets their specialty, but most dedicated "comet watchers" are amateur astronomers. They make it their goal to find new comets, and they often succeed!

Lists of the known comets with regular orbits and when they can be seen are available from observatories or from the astronomy departments of universities. If you do not live near one of these sources, write to the Smithsonian Astrophysical Observatory, Cambridge, Massachusetts 02138 and ask for the information you need.

At these places, too, you will find other people who share your interest in comets. You can search for comets together or at least compare your notes and observations from time to time.

Very large, bright comets can be seen with the naked eye, of course, but there are few of this sort. At the time of their discovery, most are spotted by using binoculars or small telescopes. A wide field of view and low power are best. They allow for the searching of a larger portion of the sky.

If you are working alone, select a part of the sky to search and then sweep across the area slowly and carefully with your binoculars or telescope. If nothing is seen on this first sweep, make a second one. Overlap the first area you scanned to make certain you did not miss any part of the sky. As a rule, you will be able to see comets most easily just after dark in the western sky or just before daybreak in the eastern sky.

How can you tell if what you have seen is really a comet? The sky is filled with many clusters of softly glowing objects. If you find such an object and cannot identify it, check a sky atlas of the specific area where you are looking to determine whether the object is charted. If it changes its position in relation to those around it within an hour or two, then there is a good chance that you have found a comet. If it is clear enough for you to detect a tail, then you can be more certain, of course. But few comets are close enough when first observed to see their tail—if they have one.

You can make a record of your observation and also get a more positive check on whether or not it is a comet by taking a photograph. Large and very bright comets can be photographed directly, without a telescope. A picture will actually show the comet more clearly than you can see it with your eyes, even through binoculars or a telescope. For taking pic-

COMETS OF THE 1980s

Name	Period or Orbit (in years)	Last Seen	Expected Return	Discovery	Observed Returns
Encke	3.3	1980	1983	1786	52
Grigg-Skjellerup	5.1	1977	1982	1902	8
Temple 2	5.3	1977	1982	1873	12
D'Arrest	6.2	1976	1982	1851	10
Pons-Winnecke	6.3	1976	1982	1819	18
Kopff	6.4	1977	1983	1906	11
Giacobini-Zinner	6.5	1978	1984	1900	7
Faye	7.4	1977	1983	1843	14
Schaumasse	8.4	1976	1984	1911	7
Halley's	76	1910	1985	240 B.C.	30

tures through your telescope, you will need an adapter. You can buy one at most stores that sell telescopes and other sky-observation equipment, or you can get directions there for making an adapter inexpensively.

How successful might you be at finding comets? Using a homemade telescope, a man who worked as a janitor in an observatory discovered twenty-eight comets during his twenty-seven years of searching for them. Another amateur observer discovered twenty-five. Still another found twenty-two. But the record goes to J. L. Pons, a Frenchman, who has the discovery of thirty-seven comets to his credit.

Of the comets listed on the preceding page, only Halley's Comet is expected to attain naked-eye visibility between now and the end of the century. Others, such as Encke's, should be visible with a small telescope. No other comets are expected to become really bright during this century, but no one knows what discoveries might be made. Kohoutek's Comet, for example, made an unexpected visit in the 1970s.

CHAPTER FIVE

WHAT ARE METEORS?

Comets ride majestically across the heavens. Meteors race! They are the flashes of light that most people call "falling stars."

Meteors come many miles closer to the earth than do comets. They travel only some 20 to 70 miles (32 to 112 km) above the earth's surface. Moving at speeds of around 20 miles (32 km) per second, and often much faster, their outer layers, or the particles cast off from them, ignite or "glow," due to friction, as they pass through the heavy atmosphere that surrounds the earth.

WHERE AND WHEN TO LOOK

You can see a meteor on almost any night, but the darker the night, the better. If you are looking specifically for meteors, get as far away from bright streetlights as possible. Somewhere away from a city is best. A few days before and after a new moon are good, too, for at these times the sky is the darkest. The best time for looking is after midnight.

Meteor simply means "something in the air." Specifically, it refers only to the flash of light, or "shooting star," seen in the sky. Remember, it is the darkness of the night that ordinarily makes meteors visible, but they do not "come out" only at night. Meteors are no less abundant during the day. Falls of large objects also cause an intense light in the daytime, and if you are close enough to them, you will see that light. Those who have been near enough say the light is suddenly brighter than the sun's and behind the light is a huge trail of smoke and dust.

SIZE AND BRIGHTNESS

Most meteors are tiny dustlike particles, but even ones that small make amazingly bright streaks across the sky. Depending on their temperature and composition, their color may be white, yellow, blue, green, orange, or red. The very brightest are called *fireballs*. The specific measure of what makes a meteor a fireball is disputable. One astronomer says that any meteor bright enough to be written up in the newspaper qualifies as a fireball. All agree that fireballs are so bright that they can be seen for hundreds of miles. They are even brighter than the brightest planets—Venus and Jupiter—when these are in their closest positions to the earth.

Fireballs that explode in the air are called *bolides*. Bolides are rare. The explosion is brought about when the outside of the body becomes so much hotter than the cold interior that extreme pressures are created. The noise of the explosion can be heard at a distance of a hundred miles (160 km) or more.

METEOROIDS AND METEORITES

The fact that metal and stone objects really do fall from the sky has been recognized only recently. Although meteorites were found in ancient times, there was much skepticism that these objects really came from the sky. Religious leaders suggested that they had been cast down in anger from the heavens. They called the meteorites "messengers of the gods" and used their

A 1966 Leonid Fireball

—36

sudden appearances to frighten people into taking religion more seriously. In contrast, some early scientists suggested that these unusual rocks were just earth rocks that had been struck by lightning.

Scientists estimate that as many as 100 million meteoroids enter the earth's atmosphere every day. Most are extremely small, no larger than a grain of sand. Some are large and can even weigh tons. Those that do not burn up as they race through the atmosphere fall to the earth. These are the meteorites. The very smallest meteorites are known as *micrometeorites*.

All meteorites contain at least some metal. This distinguishes them from almost all the other rocks found on the earth's surface. They generally belong to one of three categories: iron, stony, or stony irons. Iron meteorites resemble what the earth's core is believed to consist of. Stony meteorites are much like the rocks deep beneath the earth's surface.

These facts have led some scientists to suggest that meteorites may represent the breakup in space of another earthlike planet or other body that was similar in nature to the earth. Other scientists have suggested that meteorites were formed at the creation of the solar system out of material that simply never combined to form a planet.

Iron meteorites, or *siderites*, are the best known. They generally consist of about 90 percent iron. Before it was learned how to extract iron from ores in which it was combined with other elements, the few iron meteorites found were greatly prized as sources of this rare metal. Indeed, *iron,* an ancient word that means "metal from heaven," was once considered as valuable as gold and silver.

About 9 percent of an iron meteorite consists of nickel. The remaining 1 percent is a combination of platinum, gold, silver, and other metals. None are in amounts large enough to be of significance, though.

Stony meteorites, or *aerolites*, are dark stones that contain

A Kansas meteorite,
found in 1936

large amounts of oxygen in combination with magnesium, iron, silicon, calcium, and other elements. Olivine and pyroxene are the two most abundant minerals in stony meteorites. Some contain tiny diamonds, and others have radioactive elements such as uranium. These radioactive elements make it possible to determine the age of a meteorite.

Stony irons, or *siderolites*, are the third and rarest type. They are made up of about equal parts of metal and rock.

A fourth type of object that has been found in many parts of the world may also be a type of meteorite. Called *tektites,* these objects resemble glass. None of those found weighs more than about 2 pounds (.9 kg). Once they were believed to have come from the moon, but this theory was discarded as a result of the *Apollo* moon missions. Another theory suggests that they may have been produced by the impact of very large meteorites on the moon or earth. At this time, the precise origin of tektites remains a mystery.

Scientists are greatly interested in the composition of these various missiles from the heavens. They are often referred to by those who study them as "Rosetta stones from space." The field of "meteoritics" has grown tremendously in recent years. With special cameras and instruments, some scientists photograph meteors in motion. One instrument, the *spectroscope,* can determine the composition of the meteor.

Meteorites that have been lying on the ground for some time are generally weathered. But now and then one is recovered almost immediately after it hits. Those that have been on the ground for an undetermined length of time are called *finds*. Some finds have been on the earth's surface for many hundreds or even thousands of years. The meteorites recovered almost immediately are called *falls.* Of the more than 2,000 meteorites discovered so far, most are finds.

It is interesting that no brand-new elements have been found in meteorites. In other words, they are chemically identical to matter on the earth. This may indicate that the earth and meteorites share a common origin.

ANTARCTICA'S METEORITES

Several thousand meteorites have been found recently in Antarctica. Of particular interest to scientists are those discovered in an area some 200 miles (320 km) north of McCurdo Sound, the site of a U.S. research station.

Ninety-eight percent of Antarctica is covered with ice. As a result, the meteorites that fall there become frozen immediately after they land. When recovered, they are treated very carefully. Even though these meteorites may have been on earth for countless thousands of years, they have usually been well preserved by the ice or cold, dry conditions.

Recently, some scientists have also begun dredging the ocean floor for meteorite specimens. Of the approximately 500 meteorite falls each year worldwide, only about 150 come down on land.

Dr. Cyril Ponnamperuma, a scientist at the University of Maryland, has been one of the chief investigators of the meteorites from Antarctica. In some of them he has found amino acids. Amino acids are the basic protein compounds that are essential for life. Some of the amino acids found in the meteorites differ from those found on earth. Dr. Ponnamperuma says these compounds are "clearly extraterrestrial and pre-biotic," which means that they come from outer space and are the forerunners of life rather than fossils of once-living things.

The discovery of amino acids in the meteorites has revived a theory of many years ago. This theory said that life on earth did not originate by a combination of chemicals in the sea nor in a primordial swamp. Rather, it came from sporelike forms that dropped onto the earth from the heavens. Scientists who propose this idea say that new forms of primitive life may still be arriving today. Obviously, they are not large or fully developed forms, such as elephants or oak trees. But if the idea has any validity at all, it may explain the sudden emergence of some deadly microscopic forms of life that cause epidemic diseases among humans and other living things. So far, of course, this idea is pure speculation.

CHAPTER SIX

GIANT MISSILES FROM THE SKY

As far as anyone knows, with the possible exception of the Tunguska incident (see pp. 45–49), throughout human history no comet has ever collided with the earth. But with meteors, the rain of materials to the ground is constant. And occasionally, the meteors that fall are giant hunks that crash into the earth and create huge *craters*. About seventy such craters have been found in various parts of the world to date.

METEOR CRATER

One of the world's most famous meteorite craters is near Winslow, Arizona. The crater measures 4,200 feet (1,260 m) across and is nearly 600 feet (180 m) deep. It is big enough to hold nearly all of midtown Manhattan. The force with which the meteorite crashed must have been tremendous. It lifted the rocks around the crater more than 100 feet (30 m) above the surrounding desert—and some of these rocks weighed more than 6 tons!

The giant crater may have been formed by a single huge meteorite or by a swarm of smaller ones all hitting at the same time. About 30 tons of small iron meteorites have been found in and around the crater, but no large ones have thus far been discovered. If one did exist, it must have vaporized, which experts say is typical of meteorites that weigh 100 tons or

Meteor Crater, near Winslow, Arizona

more. Scientists have probed the crater many times. They have even drilled shafts thousands of feet deep into the area around it, thinking that a large meteorite might have slid into the earth at an angle. To date they have made no significant discoveries.

It is estimated that the crater is roughly 25,000 years old. Today it is a government-operated tourist attraction. Thousands of people visit it annually to see the gigantic chasm created by this visitor from the heavens.

OTHER CRATERS

An even larger crater was found in Quebec in 1950. It measures more than 2 miles (3.2 km) across, and its depth exceeds 800 feet (240 m). Most of it is now occupied by a lake. Was this huge crater caused by a meteorite or by volcanic activity? Scientists have not decided yet.

Several craters in Australia were unquestionably caused by meteorites. There are more than a dozen, for example, at Henbury, and others are at Wolf Creek, Boxhole, and Dalagaranga. Still more have been found in Texas, Arabia, Africa, and Argentina, which confirms that some meteors do not burn up completely but instead reach the earth intact.

LOST CITY, OKLAHOMA

It happened on January 3, 1970. A flash of light momentarily lit up the snow-covered fields of this small community, and then, just as suddenly, it was gone. Few people concerned themselves about the light. But some state policemen and a group of local residents set out to investigate.

What they found was a one-ton rock that had hurtled through the atmosphere. Fragments of the meteorite were sent immediately to the Smithsonian Institution in Washington, D.C., for analysis. Later, still more fragments were found in the area. It is analysis of such falls that continues to contribute to our understanding of the solar system and its components.

WHAT HAPPENED IN SIBERIA?

Two notable falls occurred in Siberia in recent times. Both were witnessed by people in the area. The first was in an isolated spot near the Tunguska River early on the morning of June 30, 1908. About 40 miles (64 km) from the fall, a man saw a dazzling, bluish-white fireball. It was even brighter than the sun, he said. Then, almost immediately, he felt a strong wave of hot air. He was literally blown off his feet and hurled to the ground. Windows of houses 40 miles (64 km) away were blown inward by the blast. Five miles (8 km) from the fall site, a whole herd of reindeer was totally annihilated. The sound of the blast was so loud that it was heard for some 600 miles (960 km) around. Trees were torn out of the ground. The few that were left standing became charred and lifeless poles. In all, about 1,100 square miles (2,860 sq km) of forest were devastated. Tons of dust hung in the air for months afterward. The dust absorbed and reflected the light of the sun, even when it was below the horizon, so the nights remained almost as bright as the days.

Because of the remoteness of the area, almost twenty years passed before scientists visited it to investigate what had happened. What they found led some to speculate that the temperature in the immediate area may have been as high as 30 million degrees Fahrenheit (17 million degrees C) and that the blast was probably equal to 30 million tons of dynamite. This is roughly 1,500 times more powerful than the blast from the bomb dropped on Hiroshima, Japan, near the end of World War II.

Since no meteorite fragments were found, some scientists were not convinced that the blast had really been caused by a meteorite. But meteorite dust was found in the area. This seemed to indicate that the body, if it had been a meteorite, had been extremely large and fragile and must have vaporized on impact. Another theory, one which has found wide accep-

*Site of the 1908 Siberian explosion,
possibly caused by a comet or
a meteorite. This photograph shows
trees felled by the blast.*

tance lately, is that Siberia was hit by a small comet, the nucleus of which was vaporized as it sped through our atmosphere.

Scientists recently developed a computer model of the explosion. They reported that as much as 30 million tons of nitric oxide would have been generated in the upper atmosphere by the blast. Nitric oxide reacts readily with ozone, a type of oxygen found in the upper atmosphere. The amount of nitric oxide produced would have been enough to drain roughly 45 percent of the ozone from the atmosphere, and the effect would have continued for at least three years. Researchers are not certain just what effect this might have had on the earth's climate, but they do note that there was a general cooling over the northern hemisphere during the ten years following the explosion.

Speculations about the Tunguska cataclysm continue. Some people say it was not a meteorite or comet at all but a spacecraft that came from another planet. Others say it was an alien spacecraft taking off from earth or a missile aimed at earth from a distant planet. It has even been suggested that the earth was really struck by a small black hole, a collapsed star with gravity so strong that theoretically not even light can escape from it. Most scientists are convinced, however, that the explosion was caused by impact with either a comet or a meteorite.

Who would have ever believed that almost the very same thing would happen again in almost the very same area? Well, it did.

On February 12, 1947, another object hurtled through space and fell to the earth in the Sikhote-Alin mountain region of Siberia. Again the light was blinding, and the huge white fireball was followed by a long trail of smoke. Then came a series of explosions that were very much like artillery fire.

Pilots set out to locate the impact area. They discovered more than a hundred craters, some of them quite large. From

the air, the craters were easily identified as rust-colored holes in the pure white snow covering the tundra. Scientists then visited the area and found iron fragments. Most of those who investigated the incident were convinced that in this case, at least, the object was a tremendous meteoroid that broke into fragments as it passed through the earth's atmosphere.

THE HOBA AND
CAPE YORK IRONS

The largest meteorite found to date is the Hoba Iron in southwestern Africa. It weighs 60 tons, yet because it struck a solid base of limestone, the huge meteorite sank only about 5 feet (1.5 m) into the earth. It still lies where it fell, around the year 1920, and because it is composed largely of iron, it is rusting. Some scientists have estimated that its original weight may have been as much as 80 tons.

Found in Greenland, the Cape York (or Ahnighito) meteorite was moved to the American Museum of Natural History in New York City where it is now on display. It weighs slightly more than 34 tons, and like the Hoba meteorite, it consists mainly of iron.

STONE METEORITES

Large stone meteorites are much less common. They apparently break up more easily as they pass through the earth's atmosphere. Therefore, they usually do not reach the ground in single big chunks. But a 2-ton stone meteorite fell in Manchuria, China, in 1976, and another weighing a ton fell in Kansas in

Top: *the Cape York meteorite, now in the American Museum of Natural History in New York City.* Bottom: *the discovery of the Hoba Iron in southwestern Africa*

—*49*

1948. Peculiarly, Kansas has been hit by an especially large number of stone and stony-iron meteorites. Some eighty have been recovered there to date. Compared to other areas in the world of similar size, this number is extremely high.

THE ALLENDE METEORITES

One night in February 1969, more than 100 square miles (260 sq km) of the earth near the Allende Valley in northern Mexico was showered with an estimated 2 tons of stone meteorites. The fireball from which they came was seen as far north as Texas and New Mexico. The number of falls recovered was the largest in history, and scientists declared them to be "the most primitive and the most complex" ever obtained. They are still being studied.

"These are crumbs and scraps left over from the formation of the solar system," one scientist explained.

The Allende meteorites had never been part of a larger body, such as a planet. Rather, they were formed at the same time and from the same sorts of materials as our solar system. Meteorites like these are called *chondrites,* because they contain small round bodies (chondrules) of a silicate material believed to be as old as the solar system. They also contain small white bodies that at first confounded scientists.

By radioactive dating, the Allende meteorites were determined to be 4.6 billion years old—the age of the solar system itself. And analysis of the mysterious white inclusions revealed that they were rich in calcium, aluminum, and titanium. These are precisely the elements that scientists said would be the first to condense from the swirling cosmic dust that gave rise to the solar system.

The Allende meteorites are changing our ideas on how the solar system came into being. For a long time, astronomers have believed that the solar system formed as the result of a collapse of interstellar dust and gas. But they haven't been able to determine just what caused the collapse. Now, from exami-

The site of the Allende meteorite fall

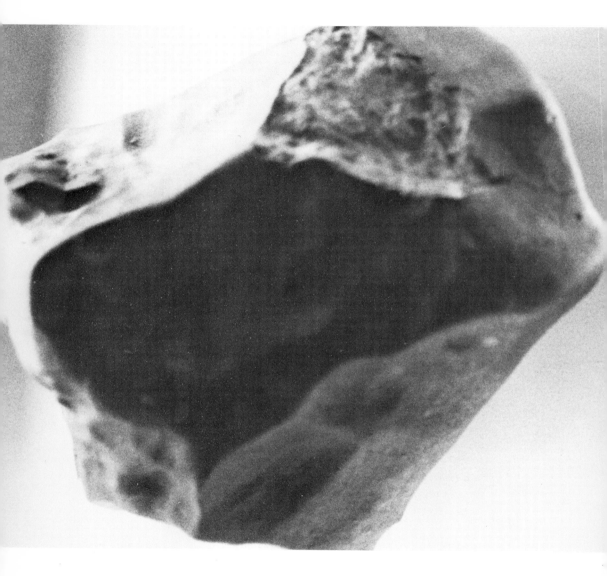

*A chondrite meteorite,
which fell in Modoc, Kansas,
on September 2, 1905*

nation of the elements that make up the Allende meteorites, especially a form of magnesium that comes from radioactive aluminum, they believe that a nearby supernova might have been the cause.

A supernova is a giant star explosion. A by-product of this explosion is radioactive aluminum. The shock wave from such an explosion could conceivably have triggered the contraction of the gas cloud, leaving remnants of the exploded star in the oldest materials in our solar system, the chondrite meteorites.

Thus, the Allende meteorites have added greatly to the knowledge we have about the solar system and its formation, and with similar findings in Antarctica, are providing clues to the origin of life itself.

METEORITES IN HISTORY

Meteorites do not have a distinctive shape or form. In this respect, they are indistinguishable from other rocks found on the earth's surface. But all through recorded history they have fascinated people. Swords and daggers were fashioned out of the iron meteorites, because it was believed that their "heavenly" origin gave the weapons supernatural power. The sacred black stone mounted in silver in the Kaaba, the holiest place of worship in Mecca for Mohammedans, is a meteorite. According to legend, the black stone was given to Abraham by the angel Gabriel. It is also said that the stone was first white and that it turned black due to the sins of man.

YOUR CHANCES OF BEING HIT

What are the chances of a meteorite falling on you or near where you live? Except for the tiny particles that come down all the time, the chances are slim. Based on statistics, a meteorite strikes a human only once every 10,000 years. A number of historical accounts of deaths due to "stones" from the sky have been found, but none have been verified. Only one person is known to definitely have been hit by a meteorite. That incident is described in the first chapter of this book.

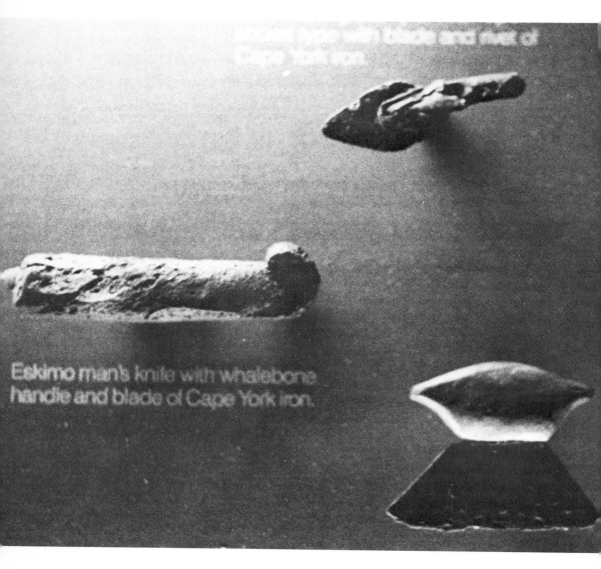

Eskimo knife with blade and rivet of
Cape York iron.

Eskimo man's knife with whalebone
handle and blade of Cape York iron.

*Eskimo tools made from pieces
of the Cape York meteorite*

Direct hits are referred to in the Bible, however, in Joshua 10:11: "And it came to pass, as they fled from before Israel, and were in the descent to Beth-Horon, that the Lord cast down great stones from heaven upon them unto Azekah, and they died: there were more which died with hailstones than they whom the children of Israel slew with the sword."

If this was indeed a shower of meteorites, as some students of the Bible believe, it is the only multiple killing by meteorites in recorded history.

NEAR MISSES

No one really knows how many meteoroids may have come close to hitting people and then missed. One near miss was observed by a satellite in 1972. The meteoroid was estimated to have weighed about a thousand tons, and a direct hit would have been equal to the explosion of a nuclear bomb. Fortunately, the body raced across the sky and never came closer to the surface of the earth than 37 miles (58.2 km). Then it disappeared in space.

And now we have man-made meteoroids to consider. Some 4,500 pieces of orbiting hardware hurtle through space today. Some of these objects are functional satellites controlled by space stations on earth. Others are the debris, or "junk," left over from human exploration or the utilization of space. Occasionally a piece of this hardware drops low enough to be slowed by the friction of the earth's upper atmosphere, causing it to plummet into the lower atmosphere. Heated by the friction, most of the objects burn up totally before reaching the ground.

Chicken Little screamed, "The sky is falling! The sky is falling!" And on July 11, 1979, everyone was watching the skies to see if her warning would come true. What was all the commotion about?

After months of speculation about where and when it would occur, the giant U.S. space station Skylab ended six years in orbit and fell to the earth. It made a fiery reentry that showered tons of debris on Australia's "outback" country and gave those who observed the event an unparalleled show.

This was not the first such occurrence, although none of the previous ones received as much attention. Once, a portion of a Soviet satellite fell into a street intersection in a Wisconsin city. Portions of a U.S. spacecraft landed on the deck of a German ship in the Atlantic. And a nuclear-powered Soviet space vehicle fell to earth in the Canadian wilderness. Fortunately, no one was injured in any of these instances.

But there will be more falls. We are literally polluting the skies with man-made meteoroids, and the crowding of space has just begun. It is inevitable that a percentage of them will fall back to earth.

Meteoroids do bombard spacecraft, of course. Fortunately, there have been no major collisions so far. This was a prime concern of space pioneers in the 1940s and 1950s, when the conquering of space was still mostly in the discussion stage. Eventually, shields were developed that enabled a spacecraft to vaporize particles before they could penetrate the craft's outer shell.

CHAPTER SEVEN

WHERE DO METEORS COME FROM?

Meteoroids occur in vast numbers throughout the solar system. Many, and particularly those that cause showers, are believed to result from the disintegration of comets. Each time a comet passes near the sun, it loses some of its frozen gases. The comet's more solid matter—rocks and metals—remain in orbit and become meteoroids. Whenever the earth passes through the orbit of a disintegrated or disintegrating comet, we experience *meteor showers*.

Other meteoroids, especially the large ones, are believed to have been asteroids that strayed out of orbit and were then drawn toward the earth. Sometimes called planetoids, the asteroids are a group of minor planets that orbit the sun between Mars and Jupiter. Most astronomers believe that the asteroids formed from the original matter of the solar system, but because they were close to Jupiter, with its immense gravity, they were unable to join together to form a large planet.

Most of the asteroids are very small. Ceres, which was discovered first, is the largest. Its diameter is nearly 600 miles (960 km). Asteroids that wander out of orbit are believed to become some of the "shooting stars," or meteors, that we see from earth.

DID A METEORITE
KILL OFF THE DINOSAURS?

One group of scientists has suggested that it was a giant meteorite—probably an asteroid or at least a large portion of one—that brought about the extinction of the dinosaurs some 60 million years ago. Walter Alvarez of the University of California and some of his colleagues say the earth was once struck by an asteroid that was probably 6 miles (9.6 km) or more in diameter. The force of such an impact would have been unbelievably great. It would have created a crater roughly 100 miles (176 km) in diameter.

Where then is this crater? No one knows. If it exists, it has yet to be located. But perhaps the very immensity of it, and the passage of millions of years, makes its location difficult to identify.

Scientists who promote this theory say that the dust rising from such a collision could block out much of the sunlight hitting the earth for as long as five years. Without this light, many plants would die, and the animals that depended directly on these plants for food would die, too. Then the predators of these animals would die. Only those creatures that could survive on dead remains or on spores or other long-lasting plant parts could survive such a gigantic catastrophe. Normal living conditions would resume only when the dust from the gigantic explosion finally settled and the sun began to shine normally again.

It is true that in the period of the earth's history when this collision is said to have occurred, about 75 percent of all species of plants and animals disappeared. Among the notable victims were the giant dinosaurs, the largest creatures ever to have walked the earth. With them went nearly all of their close reptilian kin.

How did the scientists come up with the meteorite theory? In rock samples dating back to the time of the extinction of the dinosaurs, scientists have found extraordinarily large amounts of iridium. Iridium is an element that is uncommon in earth's ordinary rocks but which is much more abundant in samples of matter from space. This led to the conclusion that some huge extraterrestrial object had struck the earth at that time.

Other scientists have since analyzed additional rock samples from various parts of the world. They have confirmed that the samples from that particular period of earth's history do contain remarkable amounts of iridium, which corresponds to the amounts normally found in meteorites. Still, other theories on the disappearance of the dinosaur have been offered, but as yet, none has been completely accepted by the scientific community.

Could such a disaster happen again? Yes. But statistically, we appear to be safe for at least another 35 million years.

CHAPTER EIGHT

LOOKING FOR METEORS

About 200,000 meteors a day are visible worldwide. Some people make "meteor watching" their hobby. Those who are serious about it generally prefer to work in groups of four or more. They lie on the ground in a circle with their feet at the center. Each body becomes like a spoke in a wheel, and each person has a commanding view of a quarter of the sky. No part is missed. They do not use binoculars or telescopes, since these would only be a hindrance.

Generally, each group also has a "clerk" to record what is reported—the specific location, degree of brightness, and direction of any meteor seen. Reports of half a dozen or more meteors per hour are not at all uncommon where an intensive search of this sort is made. Usually, however, fewer are seen. The best time to watch is from 11:00 P.M. to just before dawn.

Suppose you are among the fortunate few to see a meteor streak all the way to the ground. What should you do?

First, make a note of precisely when you saw the meteor, even to the minute. Also note how long it was seen in the sky and its brightness and color.

Was there a noise?

Did you see smoke or dust?

At a fall site, make notes about the size of the hole or depression made by the meteorite. Interestingly, some sizable meteorites do not make holes or depressions at all. They are found lying on the surface and are indistinguishable from other surface rocks.

If you do find a meteorite that has just fallen and you pick it up, note whether it feels hot, warm, or cold. Surprisingly, most are cold or only slightly warm to the touch. The exterior glows at first from being heated-up during the meteorite's high-speed travel through the atmosphere, a trip that usually lasts only a few seconds.Then the outside will quickly begin to cool off. The interior will remain deeply frozen for a while, as it was in space. This is easier to understand if you think of an ice cube in your hand. The cube's outside melts and becomes watery and warm, but its inside is still cold and solidly frozen. Occasionally a meteorite will become covered with frost after it lands, as a result of its frozen interior.

All meteorites have what is called a *fusion crust*. This is the thin outer portion of the meteor that was heated as the object fell through the atmosphere. The crust on iron meteorites is usually black or black with a bluish tinge. In contrast, the crust on stony meteorites is usually red or brownish. After the meteorite has been on the ground for a while, this outer crust becomes weathered and sloughs off.

What should you do if you see a meteorite fall? Report it immediately to the nearest observatory, museum of natural history, or university astronomy department. If there are no observatories, museums, or universities near where you live, then call or send the information to one of the following:

Smithsonian Institution
14th and Constitution Avenue, NW
Washington, D.C. 20560

Center for Meteorite Studies
Arizona State University
Tempe, Arizona 85281

Institute of Meteorites
University of New Mexico
Albuquerque, New Mexico 87131

Most spectacular, of course, are the swarms or showers of meteors in which many thousands of objects may be observed every hour. Some of these showers can be seen about the same time every year. Therefore, it is possible to know to the day when to expect them and where to look for them in the sky. During some years, the showers are truly breathtaking. As mentioned earlier, we see the displays only at night, when the sky becomes dark. But the objects continue to speed through the sky even during the day. With radar, meteor trails can be picked up at all times, even when they are not otherwise visible or detectable.

The apparent point of origin for a meteor shower is called its *radiant,* and the shower itself is named for its apparent location. The Perseids, for example, appear in the region of the constellation Perseus, and they are seen every year in August.

The Leonids provide another large and reliable set of showers. During the Leonid showers of November 1966, as many as 60,000 meteors were recorded in an hour—even more than during the 1833 extravaganza. The peak of the 1966 spectacle occurred just before dawn, and the excited observers agreed that the shower became, at that time, a literal storm of flashing lights in the sky.

The Great Leonid
Meteor Shower of 1966

—62

SOME REGULARLY OCCURRING METEOR SHOWERS

Name	When	Date of Maximum Activity	Where	Sightings per hour
Quadrantids	Jan. 1–6	Jan. 4	between Boötes and the head of Draco	100+
Lyrids	April 19–24	Apr. 22	between Vega and Hercules	12+
Aquarids (may be related to Halley's Comet)	May 2–7	May 5	south of the square of Pegasus	20
Perseids	July 25–Aug. 13	Aug. 12	in area of Perseus	68
Draconids	Oct. 8–11	Oct. 10	seen about every 6½ yrs; often very bright; should be seen in 1983 and again in 1989	54
Orionids (may be related to Halley's Comet)	Oct. 15–26	Oct. 22	between Orion and Gemini	24
Taurids	Oct. 20–Nov. 30	Nov. 8	in vicinity of Taurus	12
Andromedids (may be related to Biela's Comet)	Nov. 15–Dec. 6	Nov. 27	in vicinity of Andromeda	very low
Leonids	Nov. 15–Nov. 22	Nov. 18	in constellation Leo	20
Geminids	Dec. 7–Dec. 15	Dec. 14	in Gemini, particularly near Castor	58

GLOSSARY

Aerolite—a meteorite consisting largely of stone, mainly oxygen in combination with magnesium, iron, silicon, and calcium. Some aerolites contain tiny diamonds.

Aphelion—the point in orbit where a body is farthest from the sun.

Bolide—a fireball, or very bright meteoroid, that explodes in the air.

Chondrite—a meteorite that contains small rounded bodies (chondrules) of silicate material that may be as old as the solar system itself.

Coma—the gaseous portion of a comet's head.

Comet—a collection of frozen gases and solid debris (rocks and metals) traveling in orbit around the solar system.

Cosmic dust—meteorites dustlike in size that fall to the earth by the tons every day.

Crater—the depression made by the fall of a large meteorite.

Fall—a meteorite recovered almost immediately after it hits the ground; these are rare.

Find—a meteorite recovered many years after it reaches the ground; these are the most common kinds.

Fireball—a very bright meteor that can be seen for hundreds of miles.

Fluorescence—the emission of light due to absorption of radiation from another source.

Fusion crust—the thin outer portion of a meteorite that is heated as the object travels at great speed through the atmosphere.

Head—the nucleus and coma of a comet.

Meteor—a streak of light in the sky caused by the passing of a meteoroid through the atmosphere.

Meteorite—a solid stony or metallic object that falls onto the earth without burning up while passing through space.

Meteoroid—a solid object traveling through space at great speed; those that enter the earth's atmosphere burn up, and their bright streaks are called meteors.

Meteor shower—meteors seen in the sky whenever the earth passes through the orbit of a comet that is breaking up.

Micrometeorite—a very small meteorite, usually smaller than a grain of sand.

Nucleus—in a comet, refers to the solid particles (rocks, dust, metals, and frozen gases) that form the inner portion of the head.

Orbit—the track or path followed by an object as it travels around a larger, more massive body; the course is generally elliptical, or egg-shaped, but may be round or irregular.

Perihelion—the point in orbit when a body is closest to the sun.

Period—the time it takes for an object to complete one orbit around another body.

Periodic comets—comets that are seen regularly and are on predictable orbits.

Radiant—the apparent point of origin of a meteor shower.

Shooting star—a name commonly used in describing the streak of light made by a meteor burning up in the atmosphere.

Siderite—a metallic meteorite, consisting of about 90 percent iron.

Siderolite—a meteorite consisting of equal parts of metal and rock.

Spectroscope—an instrument used to disperse light into its various wavelengths for analysis; can be used to determine the composition of a meteor.

Tail—in a comet, the thin, trailing, and veil-like portion, sometimes hundreds of millions of miles long.

Tektite—glasslike objects, rarely weighing more than 2 pounds (.9 kg), that may be a special kind of meteorite, but the precise origin of tektites is still unknown.

FOR FURTHER READING

All astronomy books contain references and often lengthy discussions of comets and meteors. The books listed here focus on the topic and provide up-to-date information.

Ash, Russel. *Comets.* New York: Bounty Books (a division of Crown), 1978.

Asimov, Isaac. *How Did We Find Out About Comets?* New York: Walker, 1975.

Brown, Peter Lancaster. *Comets, Meteorites, and Men.* New York: Taplinger, 1973.

Heide, Fritz. *Meteorites.* Chicago: University of Chicago Press, 1957.

Jastrow, Robert and Malcolm H. Thomson. *Astronomy: Fundamentals and Frontiers.* New York: Wiley, 1972.

Kaufman, William J., III. *Exploration of the Solar System.* New York: Macmillan, 1978.

Moore, Patrick. *Astronomy Facts and Feats* (A Guinness Superlatives Book). New York: Sterling, 1979.

Murden, James. *Astronomy with Binoculars.* New York: Crowell, 1963.

Pasachoff, Jay M. *Contemporary Astronomy.* Second Edition. New York: Saunders College Publishing, 1981.

Richardson, Robert S. *Getting Acquainted with Comets.* New York: McGraw-Hill, 1967.

INDEX

ABOUT THE AUTHOR

George S. Fichter is the author of over 60 books and 300 newspaper and magazine articles, primarily in the science field. Many of his books are for young readers. For Franklin Watts, he has recently authored two popular titles in the First Book series, *The Space Shuttle* and *Disastrous Fires*.

Mr. Fichter lives with his wife in Homestead, Florida, and has three children.